How to Achieve your Goals

No Matter How Large or Small

By Jean Young

Copyright © Experience Everything Productions Inc. - All Rights Reserved

Disclaimer

This document is geared towards providing exact and reliable information in regards to the topic and issue covered. The publication is sold with the idea that the publisher is not required to render accounting, officially permitted, or otherwise, qualified services. If advice is necessary, legal or professional, a practiced individual in the profession should be ordered.

- From a Declaration of Principles which was accepted and approved equally by a Committee of the American Bar Association and a Committee of Publishers and Associations:

In no way is it legal to reproduce, duplicate, or transmit any part of this document in either electronic means or in printed format. Recording of this publication is strictly prohibited and any storage of this document is not allowed unless with written permission from the publisher. All rights reserved.

The information provided herein is stated to be truthful and consistent, in that any liability, in terms of inattention or otherwise, by any usage or abuse of any policies, processes, or directions contained within is the solitary and utter responsibility of the recipient reader. Under no circumstances will any legal responsibility or blame be held against the publisher for any reparation, damages, or monetary loss due to the information herein, either directly or indirectly.

Respective authors hold all copyrights not held by the publisher.

The information herein is offered for informational purposes solely, and is universal as so. The presentation of the information is without contract or any type of guarantee assurance.

The trademarks that are used are without any consent, and the publication of the trademark is without permission or backing by the trademark owner. All trademarks and brands within this book are for clarifying purposes only and are the owned by the owners themselves, not affiliated with this document.

Introduction

History of Setting Goals

Tip Number One: Commitment

Tip Number Two: Tracking Progress

Tip Number Three: Break Down Big Goals into Smaller Ones

Tip Number Four: Revisit and Revise Your Goal

Tip Number Five: Keep Your Eyes On The Prize

Tip Number Six: Consistency

Tip Number Seven: Let Goals Evolve

Tip Number Eight: Stay Positive, Think Positive

Conclusion

Introduction

Do you ever have that feeling where you seem to be drifting and kind of lost, despite working so hard? You are not the only one feels like nothing you have achieved seems to be worth anything. Why is this? One thing that could be causing this feeling is that you do not have a clear picture yet of what you want to do or what you want to achieve. You are just going through your daily life mechanically like a robot and it is hard to embark on a journey without having any idea of your destination.

This is the reason why setting goals is very important. When we have goals, we have a clear idea of what we want for the future and we know the things that we should be doing in order to achieve our goals. Setting goals is a process where we have a clear definition of what we want to achieve, how we are going to achieve it, and knowing where our focus should be. However, there are many things in life that can distract you from the goals that you have set which will lead you away from the path you should be taking.

Why is it necessary to set goals?

1. We have already mentioned the first one. When you have goals, you know what you should be doing to reach where you want to go. A goal that has a set time limit gives you something to work for. Setting and writing down your goals represents the desires that you have and it will also be your constant reminder of the things that you want to achieve.

2. Sometimes we get discouraged by the things that we want to achieve in life. It feels like we are trying to move mountains. But if you learn how to properly set goals, the seemingly impossible goals become reachable when you set smaller goals that lead up to your big goal.

3. When we have goals and are starting to see the little accomplishments that we unlock as we work for that goal, we start believing in ourselves. We realize that even the biggest dreams can be a reality when we work to achieve that goal.

4. Goals make you accountable for your failure. When you do not have any set goals, how would you know that you are failing? There is no way for you to compare how you were a few months ago compared to where you are now. However, when you have set goals it is easier for you to understand that what you are doing now is not working and you could have achieved more in the given time period.

5. The goals that you have reflect what you really want out of life. Why else would you spend so much of your time if it is not something that you desire? There will be instances when you do not really set the goals based on what you want. But even setting goals that may not be what you truly want will still do you some good. By doing so, you learn to realize the real thing that you want out of life or the things that you want to achieve.

7. We get to make the most out of life when we have goals. Because you have goals, you make sure that the things that you do will bring you closer to your targets. It allows you to enjoy life to the fullest and experience things you might not have otherwise thought to do.

After understanding the importance of setting goals, are you now curious about the best ways to set a goal? If you are, then that is great. We will continue the discussion by giving you information on how to properly set your goals.

The very first thing that you should do when it comes to setting goals is to come up with a picture of how you see yourself in the distant future. What do you want to do in this lifetime? When you have a clear picture of this, it is easier for you to set your goals in the different aspects of your life which will all play a role in achieving your lifetime goals. It is important that your lifetime goal is not just limited to one or two aspects of your life. Rather, it is preferred that you have a healthy balance in the various areas of your life. Take a look at the list below for a better understanding of what we mean.

- Before you retire, what are the things that you want to achieve in your career? How far should you be going to get that feeling of accomplishment?
- When it comes to your finances, ask yourself how much you should be earning at that certain age? Does this financial goal have a connection with your career goal?
- Do you feel the need to earn more degrees or train and acquire new skills that will make it easier for you to achieve the other goals that you have set?
- If you are not yet a parent, is there any chance in the future that you would like to be one? What kind of parent do you want to be?
- Do you have an artistic side of you that you want to express? If so, how are you going to achieve this?
- Are there any sports or physical activities that you want to try out? Do you want to have better health as you age? If so, including regular exercise in your daily life is necessary. Do not wait to feel the effects of aging before you start doing anything about it.
- When it comes to your enjoyment, what are the things that you want to do for pleasure? Yes, the goal of having fun in your life is also very important!

Once you have set your lifetime goals, the next thing you should be doing is setting smaller goals that you can achieve in five years which will help you achieve your lifetime goals. When you have set a five-year goal, it is time to break it down into even smaller goals: yearly, monthly, weekly and daily. All your goals should be based on the previous goals you've made and should all help you achieve your lifetime goal.

Take the time to review the goals you have made, both the lifetime goals and the short-term goals. Do these goals coincide with the way you want to live your life? If it does, then that's good. Otherwise, change the things that you feel do not belong.
Setting your goals can be a little overwhelming. We will list down a few tips for you to help you set your goals.

- Be SMART when you make your goals. This is a common mnemonic that you can follow as you set your goals. S stands for specific. M is for measurable. A means Action-oriented. R denotes relevant and T stands for Time-bound. So if one of your goals is to travel around the world, you will write it down as '*Traveled around the world by December 2025*' if you follow the SMART way.

- When you make your goals, use positive statements instead of negative statements.

- Be as precise as you can be with each goal that you make. This means including the time you are giving yourself to achieve this specific goal.

- If you have more than one goal, create a priority number for each goal. Trying to achieve too many goals at the same time can be overwhelming.

- Your goals should be realistic. It is okay to have seemingly difficult tasks or dreams as a goal as long as you know there is a way that you can attain it.

- The goals that you set should be performance related and not outcome goals.

Setting up goals is the easiest part but sticking to the goals that we make can be difficult. In the next sections you will find some tips that can help you stick to your goals in order to achieve them.

History of Setting SMART Goals

If you take a look at our history, you can easily see evidence of how ambitious man can be. Many of our ancestors have created seemingly impossible feats like building the Great Wall of China or the Great Pyramid in Egypt. This is what we human beings are all about. When we want to get something done, we get it done no matter what it takes.

So how did the concept of SMART goals come about? Research was done back in the 1960s regarding organizational performance and goal setting. In 1968, a seminal paper entitled *Toward A Theory Of Task Motivation And Incentives* was published by a man named Dr. Edwin Locke. In this paper he stated goals that have been properly set has a huge in the organizational performance.

By 1981, another man by the name of George T. Doran wrote the article *There's a S.M.A.R.T. Way to Write Management's Goals and Objectives* (1981 *Management Review*. AMA FORUM. 70 (11): 35–36) that continued the findings of Dr. Locke. He stated that management objectives and goals can be written in a *S.M.A.R.T* way. He mentioned that goals are not just some inarticulate things and that they can actually be measured when properly set.

Smart is a mnemonic that stands for:

Specific

Measurable

Attainable

Relevant

Time-bound

When you are able to achieve your goals, you feel good knowing that all the hard work and dedication has finally paid off. But before you will be able to achieve your goals, it is important that your actions are always in line with your goals. In the next few sections, you will find great tips to help you achieve your goals. Read on and you will be conquering goal after goal in no time!

Tip Number One: Commitment

For any goal to be achieved, it is important that you learn to stick to your goals. There are no shortcuts to reaching your goals. If you want to be able to travel around the world at a specific age, you need to be dedicated to the actions that you are taking to make this goal happen. You cannot exactly have that journey of your life without the right resources, right?

There are a few benefits when you make a commitment to your goal. What might these benefits be?

- When you are committed, you are able to focus better on your goals. There will always be times that you will doubt yourself. Will you really be able to reach the goal you have set? Or what about those times when you wonder if working toward your goal is worth missing out on some great activities your family and friends organized? Or what if you still want to sleep a little longer when you need to wake up early in the morning to jog so that you'll maintain a healthy body?

When doubt and fear arises, your commitment to your goal will help you get through it. Despite that feeling of fear and uncertainty, you still move forward and do what needs to be done. When you are just about to deviate from the path to your goal, your commitment will keep you right on track until the finish line!

- A person committed to their goal will work harder than most people. A single failure will not stop you from reaching your goals. Instead of giving up, you get back up on your feet and try again. Your commitment is your driving force to become better, stronger and tougher.

- Your commitment will eventually lead you to success. You may stumble and fall now but being the committed person that you are, you will get up and keep your eyes on the prize. Regardless of the many obstacles in your path, your commitment is going to be your key to reaching that success you've been aiming for.

Staying committed to your goals is easier said than done. So how do you stay committed?

1. To be able to stay committed to anything, you need to have the proper mindset. You need to be firm and one hundred percent sure about the commitment that you are going to make.

2. Having a clear picture of what you want to achieve will also help you stay committed. Having a clear picture of what will be waiting for you at the finish line is a good motivator.

3. No matter how clear you paint the picture waiting for you at the finish line, you are never going to reach it if you do not focus on what's important.

Tip Number Two: Tracking Progress

Tracking how much progress you have achieved towards your goals is just as important as setting your goals. How else would you know if you are on the right track if you do not keep track of how you are doing? But how do you keep track of your progress?

1. Give yourself some time to take a step back and think about the big picture. Do not live your life in a survival mode, living from one day to another without having any clear idea of where you should be headed. Knowing where you are now and the having the big picture of what you want to achieve is a good way for you to start tracking your progress.

2. The key to accomplishing any goal is to have good time management, especially when it is not just your work career that you want to focus on. Use a planner, an app, a calendar or whatever else is available to you that you want to use a way to plan and organize your schedule. Write specific goals for the week and month. Then write down things that you have to do on a daily basis to help you achieve that goal. You will feel good about yourself knowing that you are regularly doing things to achieve your goal. As a bonus, you also teach yourself to be more disciplined, determined and focused.

3. You will gain a lot from sharing your goals with somebody close to you like your spouse or a really good friend. The person that you confide in is a good source of encouragement and support. He or she will also remind you of your accountability when it comes to your goals.

4. When you do achieve a milestone in your goal or you achieve the goal itself, give yourself the time to celebrate this success before you move on to your next goal. Many of us fail to do this because we only look ahead. However, celebrating the little things that you have accomplished is a good way to encourage yourself and track what you have done so far.

Tip Number Three: Break Down Big Goals Into Smaller Ones

Having an ambitious dream can be inspiring and motivating. However, it can also be demoralizing and intimidating. Just thinking about the things that you need to do to reach your big dream can be quite scary and sometimes it turns off people completely. The distance between where they are now and where they want to be just seems too much. But wait, do not give up yet, because there is a way that you can make these big and ambitious goals more realistic and easier to reach. All you need to do is chunk the big goal into smaller ones that will eventually lead you to where you want to be in the future.

The big goal that you have needs to be broken down into mini goals or steps that will lead to your goal. The good thing about this is that the mini goals seem more realistic and easier to achieve and when you achieve each mini goal, you get a sense of accomplishment that could fuel your drive to reach that goal.

So how do you do it? You start the breaking down process by working backwards from your goal. Let us look at this example: having a successful business. How will you get there? You need to have great products and services as well as customers that will buy what you have to offer, right? And how are you going to get your customers? Which will then bring you to the things you need to do to reach them and how you are going to communicate with them.

Every time you set a small goal, you need to check if there is any way that you can break it down further into even smaller goals. Following this method gives you the steps that you need to take to reach your goal and what time frame you should be sticking to.
How to break down your big goals into smaller ones:

1. Make a visual map. Put the goal that you want to achieve in a circle in the middle of your paper. Then draw lines leading out from your circle where you will be listing the different things that you need to do to make your goal happen.

2. Now that you have a list of smaller tasks that you need to do, organize them into a timeline and if put together any tasks that you can do alongside each other. You need to make sure that every step that you have in your timeline is something that you can actually do and it is something that you are comfortable with.

3. Now that you have the tasks in chronological order, you need to decide how much time you need for each step. Be realistic when you make time limits and make sure that what you aim for is something that you can actually achieve.

4. What do you need to do in each step to accomplish it? Determine the actions that you need to take with every step you have listed.

5. And last but not the least, focus on the next step and not the big goal. You might get intimidated when you realize that you are still far from reaching your goal. That is the main purpose for breaking down your big goal into smaller ones, so that you do not feel intimidated by it being such an ambitious goal.

Tip Number Four: Revisit and Revise Your Goal

Every now and then, you have to revisit your goals. It is the perfect time for you to determine if the path that you are taking now is the right one. Sometimes, you only get a better picture of the whole goal setting when you have already outlined everything. If you realize that there are things that you need to change, then do not hesitate to do so. When you re-evaluate your goal, it does not mean that you are giving up. They are completely different things. When you give up your goals, you just stop pursuing them consciously or unconsciously. You give up your goals the moment you stop trying to pursue them.

Re-evaluating your goal is another thing. Did you know that re-evaluating the goals that you have already set is necessary? Just like everything else, goals also evolve. You can begin your re-evaluation of your goals by looking at the current list of goals that you have, both short and long term goals. Are there any goals there that do not mean anything to you anymore? Are these challenges that you can achieve? If so, how will you achieve them? Are there any new goals that you would like to add to your list?

When you realize that there are new goals that you want to add, you should ask yourself why you want this new goal. Do not set a new goal just because the new one is much easier for you to accomplish or you are afraid that you will not be able to achieve the goals you have already set for yourself. You should be adding new goals to your list because they are things that you really want to do. No matter how hard you try to set them aside, they won't stop bugging you until you are able to achieve them.

Having additional goals does not mean that you need to give up the goals that you have now. If for some reason the new goals creates a conflict with the goals that you currently have, try to ask yourself if you really need to make this goal happen now or is this something that you can set aside until you have accomplished your current goals.

Re-evaluating our goals is necessary for us to achieve our overall goals and sometimes even our broken down goals. Why? The circumstances of our lives change regularly and sometimes we need to adjust to this. Another benefit of re-evaluating your goals is that you are giving yourself the opportunity to focus on the goals that you want to work on and you realize which goals are not working for you. When you know which goals are no longer working for you, you can take that out from your list and focus your effort on the other goals that you want to achieve instead.

Tip Number Five: Keep Your Eyes On The Prize

There will always be days when you just want to give up. When your body and mind starts protesting from all your hard work. There will be times when you feel hopeless or even desperate. Sometimes it even feels like fate is sabotaging our attempts to make our goals and dreams happen and we just want to throw in the towel. But don't. You've worked so hard all this time, why should you give up now?

When you start getting that feeling, what should you do? You need to keep your vision burning. You need to remember the goal that you want to achieve which is the reason why you are pushing yourself to the limits. Keeping your vision alive and kicking will be motivating to you too.

So how do you keep your eyes on the prize when you feel like giving up?

1. When you start to feel that the vision is dimming right before your very eyes, remember the vision that you have for yourself, your life and your career. Write down these visions that you have on a piece of paper. It is better if you allow yourself to be as specific as possible.

2. Ask yourself why the vision that you have written down is important to you. What does it mean? Why is it important? Knowing the reason why you want to achieve your vision will be your fuel during a long journey.

3. Now that you have all this written down, spare a few minutes every morning to read what you have written down. It will be your constant reminder of your vision so that you will be able to keep it alive and, in return, it will keep you motivated as well.

When you are keeping your eyes on the prize, you will be able to:

1. Make the right decisions when necessary. There will always be days when you will find yourself at a crossroad and you are not sure what you should be doing. When this happens, keeping your eyes on the prize will help determine which path you should continue treading so that you can get your prize.

2. When you keep your eyes on the prize, you keep yourself determined and motivated to work harder and do your best to achieve that success or accomplishment that you've been keeping your eye on. A person who keeps his eyes on the prize will always emerge as victorious when it comes to success.

Tip Number Six: Consistency

Being consistent is important if you want to achieve your goals. You need to be consistent when you do your regular goal check-ins. You need to be consistent in tracking your progress. You need to be consistent on the focus, dedication and commitment that you have to achieve your goals. Even if you have created the best plan for achieving your goals, it is not going to work if you are not consistent with your actions.

How can you benefit from being consistent with your actions in achieving your goals?

1. When you are consistent with your actions, it is easy for you to determine if the action that you are taking is effective and if it will help you achieve your goal. But you need to give yourself some time before you decide if something is effective or not.

2. When you are consistent, you hold yourself accountable for any failure or success that you are achieving. If you are not getting where you should be getting then you'll know it is because you were inconsistent with your actions.

So how do you ensure that you will remain consistent at being consistent?

1. You have to consciously decide that you are going to be consistent with the actions that you have to do in order to reach your goals. Tell yourself on a daily basis that you are going to be consistent with the things that you have to do.

2. Change your concept of right now to the present time. Do not think about the day after tomorrow, the next three weeks, the next months or even the next year. Be there in the present. Focus yourself on being consistent right now in the present.

3. A plan is important if you want to be consistent. When you have a plan or goal that you want to achieve, you know that all the things that you do, your focus and your time should be dedicated to achieving your plan or goal. If you do not have that, you will find yourself drifting from one thing to another and that is not being consistent.

4. There will be times when you feel like you are not being consistent enough. But do not dwell on these negative feelings because they are only temporary. Whatever you are feeling, even if it is quite strong or overwhelming, it is going to go away in the next hours, days and weeks.

5. For you to be consistent, focus on one thing at a time. If you find yourself slowly drifting away from what you should be doing, you need to force yourself to return your one hundred focus on what you should be doing at the moment.

If none of the five tips seem to be working, there is something else that might work. If you find yourself feeling like you cannot do it because of a million reasons that you came up with, force yourself to do it anyway. No matter how sad, depressed, tired, bored, hopeless, desperate, unsure and even when you are on vacation, do it anyway if you want to remain consistent.

Tip Number Seven: Let Goals Evolve

Just like everything else, your goals will change over time too as you grow up. When you were a child, your goal was probably to be a princess, a ballerina, a doctor or even a superhero. But as you grow older you might realize that you cannot be a princess just like that, do not have the right skills to be a ballerina, you collapse at the sight of blood and being a superhero with superpowers is simply impossible.

And because you have realized that these goals are not possible, you have replaced this with another one. You want to finish school, get a great job and start a career. You also may plan to get married one day.

However, as much as we want every detail of our life planned out and to go as planned, it won't always be that way. You will encounter certain circumstances wherein you will have to change your goals in response to the changes in your life.

Do not be afraid when you realize that your goals have changed. It is completely normal and it is nothing to be freaked out about. It is not just your goals that change but so do you, over time. The things you might have been interested in before, might not be the things that interests you now. Or there might be things that you did not believe in before that you believe in now. A lot of changes can happen as time passes by. Embrace these changes and allow your goals to accommodate the new you.

Tip Number Eight: Stay Positive, Think Positive

Yes, it is already a cliché and it is tiring to hear it over and over again. But having a positive mindset and a positive attitude towards your goal will greatly impact the success that you will get from it. When you always think that you cannot do it, you are unconsciously sabotaging yourself and your actions to achieve your goals.

Below are some tips to help you maintain a positive outlook when aiming for your goals:

1. Do not allow yourself to exaggerate or think absolute thoughts. You might find yourself thinking that you always watch TV too much. Instead of saying that to yourself say this instead, *'I used to watch too much TV before but not today. I have lessened the hours I spend watching TV.'* Allow yourself to feel good when you are able to control your thoughts.

2. As soon as you can sense that negative thoughts are trying to emerge to the surface, stop them. There is always something positive and you should take some time and effort to look for the positive things especially when you are feeling really down. Look for the things that you can love and be proud of about yourself and the other people around you. Stop focusing on your negative side but concentrate on your good traits instead.

3. Every now and then, you will find yourself making a mistake or giving in to a temptation that will deviate you from your path to your goal. That's okay. What's more important is that you realize this right away, get back up on your feet and start going back to the right track. Do not beat yourself up just because you made a mistake.

4. Do not expect yourself to meet standards that you do not think anybody can achieve. Nothing is wrong with wanting to excel but it has to be realistic but challenging.

5. Encouraging yourself is a very important thing if you want to stay positive.

6. Stop feeling guilty about the things you should be doing and things you have not been able to do. Instead, concentrate on your action plan.

7. Always be a kind person to yourself.

Conclusion

If you want your life to have more meaning and want to be able to live it to the fullest then it is important that you set goals. Goals give you a sense of purpose and make your actions and your life more meaningful. However, setting big goals that you need to achieve in your lifetime can be really intimidating. But you can actually avoid all the intimidation and fear of not being able to achieve your goals by breaking down your huge goals into smaller pieces that are easier to achieve.

Trying to reach a goal, especially the more challenging ones, is not an easy task. A person who does not give it their all might not be able to achieve much. For any person to reach his or her goal, one must be dedicated wholeheartedly to a goal that they want to achieve. It is okay to make mistakes but you cannot just give up because you have an obstacle standing in your way. If you do encounter an obstacle or you find yourself drifting away from the right path to your goal, you need to make sure that you are able to focus your thoughts and actions into getting back on track. It is all about your dedication and positive outlook that will help you get back on the right path to your goals.

But before you start working to achieve your goals, it is important that you have properly set your goals using the SMART way. Having a clear outline of the things that you want to achieve at a given time can make all the difference in failing or succeeding. That, and the kind of attitude that you have.

The dreams and goals that we have now may seem unreachable. But all you need to do is take one step at a time and you'll be there in no time.

Copyright © Experience Everything Productions Inc. - All Rights Reserved

www.ingramcontent.com/pod-product-compliance
Lightning Source LLC
Chambersburg PA
CBHW070109100426
42743CB00012B/2698